Hedgehog Mountain

by Ned Pike and Freya Pike

illustrated by Luke Jurevicius

Harcourt Achieve

Rigby • Saxon • Steck-Vaughn

www.HarcourtAchieve.com
1.800.531.5015

Ruttel

Zed

DD

Contents

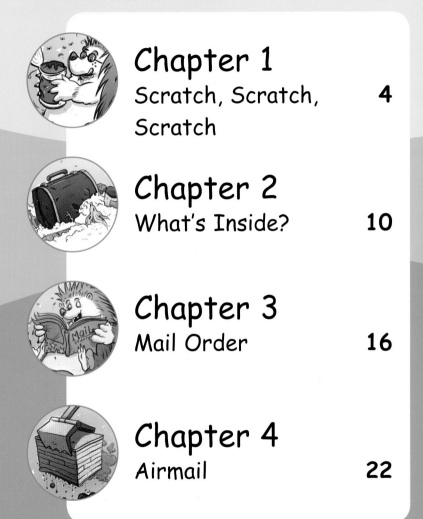

Chapter 1

Scratch, Scratch, Scratch

Life on Garbage Island was no picnic. Every day Zed, DD, and Ruttel had to look for food.

Dig, dig, dig. Scratch, scratch, scratch.

It was long, slow, smelly work. Every
night the three hedgehogs flopped
onto their beanbag chairs.

One day the garbage boat came with a
full load of trash. It was a colorful load.

"Free chocolate eggs!" cried Ruttel.
The chocolate eggs must have run
away from home. No one would throw
chocolate away. Ruttel loved chocolate.

"I wish we could get to the top of Garbage Hill," said Ruttel. "All the best food is up there."

It was true. Most of the garbage landed on top of the hill. Only a few bags rolled down to the hedgehogs.

Chapter 3

What's Inside

One day DD found a large black suitcase. Its sides bulged. It was too heavy to move. And it was locked!

DD banged the lock with his head.
The lid sprang open. The bag was full
of money!

DD had never seen money before. He picked up a ten dollar bill and ate it.

"Mmmm, not bad," he said. He sat down to eat the rest.

When Ruttel found him, DD was snacking on a pile of twenty dollar bills.

"Aaaaahhh!" Ruttel screamed. "DD, what are you doing?"

That night, curled up on their beanbag
chairs, the three hedgehogs talked.
Ruttel told Zed and DD about money
and shops.

"There are no shops on this island," said DD. "How will we buy anything?"

It was a problem.

Chapter 3

Mail Order

Ruttel dug up a mail-order catalog. He was excited. They could send away for things.

"We could buy a vacation," said Zed.

"Too clean," said DD. "What about
a tent?"

Ruttel turned the page and his eyes lit up — a camper.

They all agreed it was perfect.

So they sent away for the posh and
perfect camper. That one had little
curtains in the windows.

Since they had filled in the "send by airmail" box, a plane flew over the mountain five days later. Its belly opened, and out dropped a huge wooden crate. Even with its parachute, the crate fell fast.

It landed with a big bump next to Zed and DD. Their camper was here.

Chapter 4

Airmail

The crane near the top of the hill swung into action. The crane lifted the crate.

"It's taking our camper," shouted Zed.

"It can't! It's ours! Come on, Zed, jump on," DD cried.

23

The crate was breaking apart. Zed and DD hung onto one loose plank. The crate went higher and higher.

"Where's Ruttel?" asked DD.

Ruttel was inside the crane. "I want our new home to have a great view," Ruttel called out of the crane's window.

The crate burst open as it landed on top of Garbage Hill.

"Wow!" said DD. "We're home."

"You can see forever," said Zed.

"I name this mountain, Hedgehog Mountain." said Ruttel with a grin.

And the three of them moved in, beanbag chairs and all.

Glossary

beanbag chairs
large cushions filled with dry beans or foam balls and used as chairs

crane
a machine used to lift heavy things

crate
a wooden box

eyes lit up
felt excited and happy

hedgehogs
small mammals with sharp spines

mail-order
order and buy things and get them by mail

parachute
umbrella-shaped fabric that lets objects fall safely

posh
expensive

Ned Pike and Freya Pike

Hedgehogs make interesting pets, especially ones that are characters in a book. They don't need feeding or walking, making them super-easy to look after.

Luke Jurevicius